MAURITANIA 2.0

A NEW METHOD FOR DESIGNING A ROADMAP FOR NATION BUILDING

MAURITANIA 2.0

A NEW METHOD FOR DESIGNING A ROADMAP FOR NATION BUILDING

BY

SIDI O. SOUEINA, PHD

MAURITANIA 2.0 A NEW METHOD FOR DESIGNING
A ROADMAP FOR NATION BUILDING
Sidi O. Soueina

www.mifitt.net
Nouakchott, 2020.

Library of Congress Control Number: 2020913106

MAURITANIA 2.0

A NEW METHOD FOR DESIGNING A ROADMAP FOR NATION BUILDING

BY

SIDI O. SOUEINA, PHD

MAURITANIA 2.0 A NEW METHOD FOR DESIGNING
A ROADMAP FOR NATION BUILDING
Sidi O. Soueina

www.mifitt.net
Nouakchott, 2020.

Library of Congress Control Number: 2020913106

to Debbie.

Acknowledgements

This work would not have been possible without the help and support of many. My wife, SINOURADI, my assistant Georgette who gives so much of herself so I can have a minute to write.

Table of Contents

بسم الله الرحمن الرحيم

PROLOGUE

I HAD THE OPPORTUNITY to study, live, and work in five continents for the past twenty-five years, between 1988 and 2015. Since returning to Africa's Mauritania in 2015, I have noticed that people are incapacitated by pessimism and disbelieve that anything positive can happen here. In Africa, in Mauritania's Africa, people mainly lack the possibility of dreaming big. No more is this apparent than in the case of the COVID-19 pandemic, which started a few months ago. Many opportunities to innovate were lost, especially in education. To prove a point here is a translated Tweet, which I posted not long ago that summarises.

> *An opportunity was lost for the country to serve education in the medium term in the current Corona crisis. After weeks of reflection on the reason why schools fail in distance education, I listed a few. Two, in particular, stuck with me: vision and faith. Or rather, lack of vision and faith.*

Lack of belief that Mauritania can ever be better. Faith in Mauritania among its citizens is an old-new problem. And it seems to be more difficult for most Mauritanians to uphold.

In their claim, "Mauritania is a poor, underdeveloped country stranded in the middle of nowhere. A country, which does not deserve more than the crumbs of technology and progress. All of the innovations and meander of such tech should bear fruit in remote countries and not here," claim the pessimists. Imagine what kind of vision shall unfold post such a vision of like-minded people?

Most countries of the world switched from the pattern of brick and mortar classroom education to distance-education in weeks, at most, during the crisis. The technology is available far and wide for the rich and the poor, for the near and the far.

Pessimists do not see possibilities. They do not see the sun, and they are filled with excuses. The smallest obstacles block them, even if they see an opportunity for creativity in the first place. This is true even if it passes before their eyes in bright daylight.

If all parties seized the endless open technological and consulting opportunities available for all, there would be technical and academic advancements for education in Mauritania, which would not have been obtained in a few generations.

INSTEAD OF OUTLINING endless critiques and endless complaints, I would like to bring a small contribution. I believe that if there is a simple, clear path of understanding what is needed to be done for a country to move ahead. This path, crafted into steps and goals, besides the complex economic, social, and security theories, provides a roadmap. And if the people understand these steps well enough, the people will act upon them deliberately more so that the complex theory and pessimism will decline to allow vulnerable countries to emerge.

The idea of developing a nation using an algorithm, which is a set of steps designed to solve a problem, maybe considered far-fetched by some. But it is precisely that which made me write this book. To define an innovative, understandable, and implementable framework, tool, or a method to isolate complexity, and at the least, educate as many people as possible on what it means to be a developed nation or country and how.

This rather small book talks about unconventional ways to measure a country's success and how it is moving ahead. I say unconventional because it talks NOT about typical economic, social, and security indicators, as many have suggested. Instead, it introduces a set of six to seven steps, in the form of 'an algorithm' that will more likely guarantee the advancement of a nation when applied. When the awareness of these Seven Elements or indicators reaches a certain level in a society, the country would simply move from a 1.0 Country to 2.0 or 3.0 country, thus the MAURITANIA 2.0. These elements are One:

Belief, Two: Unifying Identity, Three: Resistance to Social Structures, Four: Practice of the Culture of Innovation, Five: Project Management Practice. Six and Seven have to do with learning the lessons and repeating the process. The direct way for such a process is to be started intentionally by a government or an entity. I hope that the book and material it contains will be a guide too, as many begin to read it, thus allowing the algorithm to take effect slowly but surely.

I am aware that there could seem to be an interpretation challenge. That is to say, to simplify such a seemingly complex issue and write it in layman non technical language. However, the hope to bring everyone to take part makes it worthwhile.

Chapter 1

THE RETURN

THE UNLIKELY DECISION to stay in Mauritania in the year of two thousand and fourteen, after twenty-five years of continuous travel was not easy to make. My travels have taken me to five continents and many countries, including Australia, Iraq, Japan, and the United States of America and Canada. I was there to study, work, and sometimes for tourism.

Apart from starting up a training and innovation institute, I've spent much time since returning to Mauritania thinking about just two things. Why are my people lagging and what to do to make a lasting and meaningful contribution to their development. This book is my attempt to try to answer the first part of the question and take part in the second. It would be most rewarding if my contribution can spread to likewise countries in Africa and around the world.

SINCE MY ARRIVAL IN MAURITANIA, I hear mostly despair and complaints across the spectrum; youth to a lesser extent, older generation, races, casts, working professionals, the unemployed, and more. What struck me the most was not the complaints. Instead, it was the inability or unwillingness of my people to dream and believe that anything but the status quo could happen.

Connected to the world now with a fiber optics cable, and in a few years-time with Elon Musk StarLink Satellite system, large parts of the country sadly still live under the same conditions as the past 60 years. It seems the past has numbed the brain and rock-solidified that within the human, which dares to dream and hope, conveniently forgetting about the wealth of possibilities of the twenty-first century. That is to say, people still have to deal with near primitive sanitation conditions, use unpaved roads, succumb to a terrible education system and a horrible health system with almost no infrastructure such as roads, dams, and bridges, and until recently an international airport.

Despite the recent limited change, when this book was drafted, in late 2016, corruption spanned the horizons of government and private sectors alike. Government and business professionals and regular citizens, seem to have fun embezzling money from the government, plotting and succeeding in ripping public projects of ALL funding, bringing fake pharmaceuticals and food products into the country, and of course, throwing trash in the streets, with little or no remorse.

Another striking trait I witnessed is the living pessimism and belief that nothing good can be done in this country or that it can move ahead. Knowing and seeing what other countries around the world have achieved does not seem to be a source of inspiration to anyone. On the contrary, it looks like it is a source of despair and further conviction that Mauritania isn't capable of pulling through nor capable of becoming anything or moving anywhere but backward!

Being a son of Africa, first and foremost, I know this is not typical of just this country.

Chapter 2

COLONIALISM & SKILLS

I **CAN THINK OF NO** causes of such conditions and traits more significant than the harsh nature in which Mauritanians lived for millennia. The social structures that Mauritanians created for themselves, the effect of colonialism on the identity of the country, and on the lack of a simple system that brings everyone together to restore the latter and treasure the former.

I know for a fact that living in such a harsh and difficult environment means constant optimism. However, in an area spanning large portions of the Western parts of the Sahara Desert, the harsh environment imposed an easily identifiable nomadic lifestyle. For centuries, we've spent most of our working hours striving to satisfy basic daily needs like getting water from the well and preparing sustenance.

Oddly perhaps enough, people have always considered reading and writing to be sacred in this country. If I am asked what the national symbol of my people is, I would say that it is a book or perhaps the Quranic tablet.

✹ ✹ ✹

SOME EUROPEAN INTELLECTUAL ELITES do not seem to understand why some Africans still talk about colonialism. French President Emmanuel Macron is one of them. For those, let me say that colonialism for many Africans is a trauma that has lived in their collective psyche for several decades. It is not a matter of hatred; it is not a matter of nationalism, but it is what people in this part of the world remember as if it happened yesterday. Just as Europeans talk about World War II and the victims, they lost as if it were 'yesterday'. This is 2020, many people I know have lost their fathers and brothers in battles, and for them, too, it is as if they perished yesterday.

THERE IS AN INTERESTING STORY of how the former French colonization came to rule Mauritania, or most parts of it anyway.

The term 'interesting,' of course, depends on who is reciting it.

It seems France was not interested in the Moor's land as one of its colonies, for most of the time it spent discovering and colonizing its neighbors in this part of West Africa. France was in Senegal and Algeria for more than two hundred years before deciding to come here.

There was a famous Sheikh (not a 'sheek', they are not the same), who decided to write a fatwa on the wrongfulness of resisting the French on the bases of ongoing slaughtering between local tribes and hoping to bring order and "justice" under the rule of France to the land.

Arabic tribes of Beni-Hassan came to the lands hundreds of years before that to the desert, and have, it seems, vastly contributed to the culture of chivalry, more like the Cherokee nomads, and the culture of the religious elites, more like the Indian Brahmans. In a vast land stretching between Niger, the Atlantic Ocean to the west, Algeria, and the Senegal River to the west was the No Man's Land. This meant chaos, death and slaughtering of the innocent. It went on for several centuries.

To this day, many still critique the Sheikh of having invited the French in, but many commend him for doing so. This book is not one-sided and can appreciate both arguments. On the one hand, why would you invite the enemy who conquered your land, to rule your people for generations to come. Especially given the fact that one could argue that the host was an elite that was well versed in the consequences of colonization and its grip. On the other, why should such an elite let his people kill each other, especially given the facts, that France was finally coming to Mauritania anyway?

I would rather conclude that colonization may still have a significant impact on the psyche of our people without having to state examples and stories such as these, something which I find rather unpleasant and difficult to recite without seeming cynical and chauvinistic.

I AM A BIG BELIEVER IN GLOBALISATION and purchasing know-how as we do airplanes, cars, and computers.

I attended a meeting back in 2017 with a newly appointed French consultant to an unnamed minister. Surrounded by six of us, professors of computer science, Mathematics, and Physics, the polite and seemingly determined Frenchman addressed us with an opening statement stating that his mission among other things was to try and make Mauritania's higher education "at least as good as Senegal or Morocco." Condescendence was all over the place. But so too was a shock, at least from one of the people present there. Ok, maybe anger as well. I almost politely replied that we should not forget that we want to be better than France. Especially since the best universities in France, including the Sorbonne, does not figure in the list of some of the most respected world university ranking systems. The only time higher education in France works is when the North American model of higher education is adopted. There is a way to become better than our neighbours and France. And that is by simply adopting one of the best models out there, such as the American model, Canadian, British, or Singaporean models. Also, the decision to do so is frankly easy to make. There is a reason why the best universities in the world are by far in quantity and quality American and, to a certain extent, Canadian.

This behavior of my friend here is not just that of someone who feels the pressure of culture-shock! It is systematically present. Mauritanians it seems, have blind faith in all that is non Mauritanian. Especially when it comes to modern systems of anything. Therefore, the condescendance I spoke about is strangely present with or without any Frenchman being there. This is a very strange phenomenon indeed. One that is inherited from the former rulers and it seems to linger and reincarnates itself again and again.

I attribute this to the widespread use of French language in the administration and of course to the colonization.

Many Mauritanians I know now feel blinded by the effects of widespread French language in their daily lives. They feel even more frustrated by the fact that in more cases than not, that frustration is expressed in French. Something that is totally insane and speaks to the identity problems I wish to address for any society to move forward.

THERE IS A SIGNIFICANT development issue with mediocre former powers that still linger in former colonies in a way or another. By mediocre I mean those which their colonization became a hindrance to development especially when compared with likewise colonies. I am referring here to a Stanford study which seems to conclude that former French colonies may be less advantageous compared to say the British. This fact has gained momentum recently with what happened in Rwanda switching from

French to English language overnight. Many speak of it as a wakeup call.

Therefore those you hear often speak about belittling former colonies in a way or another and critiquing them for not forgetting may just be exhibiting symptoms of anxiety of separation.

Let me just end here by saying that I suspect former mediocre colonizing powers will have a tougher time sustaining their models of economic development in former colonies. Those that are now connected with fiber optics to an Internet full of know-how, outsourcing possibilities, and world economic collaborations, and are all in English.

Most importantly, all information and know-how are now all over the place.

I sometimes tell my colleague professors that the new model of teaching requires one to understand that, gone is the time when the professor was the sole source of knowledge. Their roles need to become mentors, organizers, and class management heroes, and they need to develop skills in this direction. The Internet is full of know-how from simple products or service design, teaching, and designing complex projects to raising a child.

Gone is the time when the former colonising power was the source of development and know how.

Chapter 3

HOPE & LOVE OF COUNTRY

I AM A CITIZEN OF THE WORLD, literally speaking. I have lived in Iraq, Japan, Australia, the United States, and Canada. I have witnessed economies fall and rise back again in nearly most of the countries I have lived in long enough. So, to those who might want to dismiss this reasoning as being naive and unrealistic in the face of the leap that this country has to take, I would like to confirm that under no circumstances will I deny the influence of these travels on my life. However, I would like to invite them to consider that it is precisely that sort of attitude, which I think holds the key for us to get out of stagnation and backwardness. I call it not naivete, but belief. The attitude I speak about is utter optimism and belief in a bright future, in possibility, in growth, and peace.

Thus, to the amazement of some, I have indeed attempted to tackle these issues, sometimes in the tiniest possible ways, such as by discussing with a friend or family member, by writing and publishing articles or by starting a new business. Sometimes, however, by founding a conference, and indeed writing a book.

My dream is to form a team of near and far, like minded thinkers, who know no boundaries with regards to believing that something could be done and has to be done. This book is my way of identifying, connecting with them, and finally working with them through a plan depicted in the book to make things happen. The people I am talking about, have a name, have traits. But more importantly, THEY BELIEVE.

THEY LOVE Mauritania. Loving Mauritania was not a problem for these people. They are bound by identity and love for the country and its people regardless of color or cast.

THEY BELIEVE something has to be done, and something could be done. Something needs to be done starting right now.

THEY IDENTIFY with their likewise people. They are capable and willing to find other like minded people and organize with them at any level possible.

ONCE A DAY, THEY DO perform any step of the algorithm. Anything positive.

They do not listen to the nay-sayers. They know if an algorithm can guide an unmanned craft to travel for years in space and land on Mars, another can contribute to the advancement of a nation.

These are some of the most important traits of the people who will help to move this country forward.

This is the algorithm, which will be the subject of the rest of the book.

In 2015, I was invited to a conference organized by Japanese and African scholars in Ivory Coast about culture, identity, and their pertinence to emerging and developed nations. Some of the most interesting facts I learned in this conference is the significance of the identity of a country and the possibility of creating a new one if it didn't exist or if it were threatened. I knew I was on a path that could lead to having the question of why someone should love their country, answered. All we had to do is to link the personal interest to the country's identity.

When people fall in love, they care less about money and other sources of material wealth. It is the same with the love of a country. When there is love of country, the greatest desire is for the beloved country to live.

Since I hope to get as many people to identify their own identity with that of their country so that they take part in the development of their beloved country, the idea of creating a country club via writing the book came about. I hope that when reading the book, people will do the following:

- Help create, if nonexistent, a linked identity with that of their country.
- Develop optimism in the possibilities.
- Know that everything is possible and THEN fight to make it happen.

THIS WORK IS SIMPLE, and yet I hope it makes a significant contribution. If the book directly contributes to making a development revolution in this country and indeed finally moving forward on the path of emergence, that will be a real miracle. If it helps one person practicing just one element of the algorithm, then that will be enough for me.

This is not a guide per se. It is a collection of ideas and thoughts on ways to get this country moving forward.

So, what are the prerequisites for the country to be able to apply the algorithm? I might say:

1. Understanding the role past colonialism had on the identity of the people.
2. Understanding the role of ill social structures which ought to be fought.
3. Be ready for the flood of knowledge, which will come through the Internet.
4. Speak the language of the world, English.

Number 1 through three, demands no significant effort. These three depend on number four.

Chapter 4

"2.0" .. WHAT IS THAT?

THE TERM 2.0 (pronounced two-point Oh!) has become commonly used in software engineering and other disciplines to indicate that a product or service has moved from one stage to another, one phase to another, or from one version to another. In the case of this book, that country's development is going at cruise speed.

I chose to use this term for this country's development path to extrapolate the growth transformation from one defined state to another. Unlike the conventional socioeconomic indicators like GDP, I suggest using indicators linked to collective consciousness about positive psychology, unity, identity practice, and modern systems, and behavioral processes. I argue that the accumulation of such things not only signals progress but more likely sustains progress. I further suggest the use of the term X.0 to help unconventionally standardize progress. I hope that such simple terms will provide access to us all and provide an alternative that might educate and help more to understand progress and help to make everyone continue to progress and contribute.

Therefore, given this unconventional indicator, Mauritania 1.0 is pre-independence, 2.0 is where fifty percent of its people have displayed the unconventional indicators, and so on.

MAURITANIA 1.0 WAS BORN IN 1960. It was merely a country with a government, a military, radio station, and something that looked like a national anthem. There were some schools too. There are indications that the 1.0 version of it is enough demo and proof on the ground of what the country CAN DO. Since Mauritania 1.0 will come to an end soon, we hope, what should a 2.0 Mauritania look like? The primary government, education, health, and democracy are functioning smoothly. Most importantly, people are practicing democracy and freedom of expression that most tangible benefit their daily lives. 3.0 Mauritania is a regionally and internationally competitive nation.

THIS I BELIEVE is a straightforward methodology to help understand the advancement of a country to cross any X.0 threshold. Simply stated, in the last century, governments worried about the number of people who can read and write. With the Internet revolution, which effectively started at the end of the last century and is to peak, came the so-called Computer Divide, which is the difference between those who know how to use computers and those who do not. It is no longer how many people can read and write, but how many can use a PC, how many use emails, how many have social media accounts? This trend will only continue as the remaining forty percent of the world become more connected, and as technology becomes an integral part of everyday living for all.

This book argues that an accurate benchmark for how fast a country can progress will depend primarily on different indicators that we are used to. Think about how many believe in the country, how many subscribe to the unifying identity of the country, how many are aware of the social injustices and how widespread are the cultures of innovation and project management. I am not saying that the conventional indicators are to be dismissed. I am saying that the indicators I am proposing here make sense because they can be understood by all, first. Second, they would galvanize people of all walks of life to create a movement and take parts in the development.

Chapter 5

IF YOU CARE TO HELP

WHO SHOULD READ THIS BOOK? The intention behind writing this work is to provide help at my level to 'guide' you and hopefully through you, my beloved country, to reach its' greater potential in less than ten years. In addition, the book is written for citizens of the world. Government officials can use the book as a guide and universities as a textbook. The book may help in finding meaning, all the while perhaps striving for better living standards under a unified and emerging country.

This work is designed to be stripped of all unnecessary preaching and literature. The intention is to produce an easily readable text that can prepare you to participate effectively as an active individual in your social, professional, and government environments.

I AM NOT GOING TO WASTE TIME proving that the most important and most difficult fight that will have to endure to move Mauritania, or any country for that matter, forward tangibly is to convince yourself that it is possible. Knowing and acting on this basic premise is step one. Before that, nothing can happen. After it, everything is possible. Believing that it is possible is the seed from which the tree will grow. We need to start from a place. That place is a dream and a vision. We need not just to dare to dream the dream, but we need to believe it as well. Now, you might want to tell me that I am trying to change a country based on a dream. My answer is YES. I will go further and tell you that every country that shifted and moved forward started from a dream or a myth. It all starts in the virtual, first. If you want to raise a building, you dream about it. If you want to educate your children, you dream about seeing them as doctors. If you want to clean your street, you dream about seeing it clean. If you want to get rid of corruption, you dream about having none. The fight to believe in this basic premise is the most difficult fight you will endure as a father, worker, citizen, member of the government, or civic organisation. Not taking the 1% lightly, you win this fight, knowing you have done close to 99% of the work.

Now, let me tell you something about knowing how to dare to dream. It is a hint about winning in believing that it is a possible fight.

Know that pessimism is a dream killer. Know that reality is a dream killer if you look at possibilities with a pessimistic eye. Reality is a dream canvas if you look at possibilities with an optimistic but realistic attitude.

Now, you know why I decided not to waste time talking too much about the research regarding what needs to be done to move a country forward. It is obvious that when you dare to dream and be optimistic, you will attract what is needed to make it happen then. It is that simple.

The holy Qur'an says it all: "Indeed, Allah does not change that which is upon men until THEY change that which is within themselves." Not attempting to translate or interpret the Qur'an, for indeed every Ayah has seven meanings, I am tempted to project this Ayah on the issue of changing that which is upon ourselves with regards to changing our attitudes to be optimistic in the possibilities of moving our country ahead, starting now.

Also, the verse makes it clear that the responsibility of changing that which is inside of us is ON US.

Don't worry about reading the remaining chapters of this book if you are not convinced about the above fact. If you are indeed not convinced, read the previous section again and again and again. By the time you reach the seventh time, you will begin to become convinced. I hope.

Chapter 6

THE ALGORITHM

INVENTED BY A MUSLIM Mathematician called Al Khawarizmi in the twelfth century, it becames the soul of modern-day computers. It is merely a series of steps that can automatically lead to certain results. My intention in the remaining few paragraphs is to inform you, lest you were not informed, how this simple process has changed the world in the past one hundred years, faster than the remaining human history.

Before we dive into the spirit of algorithms and how they can be used to change our country for the better, let me first put on my academic hat and share a few facts about algorithms.

Fact number one pertains to the possibility of controlling the speed at which an algorithm solves a problem. An American company paid a few billion dollars to install a fiber optics cable from New York to Chicago's stock market. The aim was to have an algorithm compute the solution three nanoseconds faster. I am sharing this example so that you know how important it is to understand this phenomenon of speed when it comes to algorithms and how that can speed up our country's development plan.

Fact number two. The complexity of an algorithm isn't necessarily pertinent to the utility of the final result that we need the algorithm to deliver. An algorithm may help solve the mysteries of the Higgs Boson in CERN, where a giant microscope zooms-in to decipher the dust resulting from the smashing of two hydrogen atoms; another algorithm can be designed to add two numbers repeatedly. I'd like to argue that a third can be used to move a country forward, or inadvertently backward for that matter. One thing is sure though, the complexity of an algorithm isn't necessarily immediately pertinent to its utility. What matters is the accumulation of the final results and how that can benefit.

Finally, you may ask why? Why did I choose seven steps in this algorithm? There are seven verses in the Quran opening, the Surah "Al Fatiha." There are seven skies and seven earths. Seven-Eleven. I don't know really. I guess I just like the number seven. Plus, I repeatedly dream about myself going up a building of seven stories in an elevator. Nevermind the reason why. I'd like to convince you that it is possible to move a country forward using an algorithm of seven steps.

Before explaining the algorithm's steps and how it works, let me mention a few things that impact the performance of an algorithm. I'd like to mention only speed, variables, and cycles. Starting with the SPEED and CYCLES, the former is the amount of time an algorithm takes to finish one or more CYCLES to get the whole or part of the job done. The CYCLE is a sequence of STEPS that can be executed in time. Note, though, that some algorithms never end. This makes them perfect for our purpose as we need the country to keep moving, never-endingly. The VARIABLES are a matter of the value (that is as geeky as it gets), and it refers to certain things that the algorithm uses during the CYCLES. Things that may have changing values.

Now that we have certain basic knowledge about how algorithms change the world, let's move on to know what types of variables we need to have in our society so we can start to analyse if this algorithm might change our world?

This list contains a set of variables that I suggest we use to measure the progress of any given society towards emergence and improvements. The leadership's role (if there is one that could or cares about following up the trends proposed here) is to make sure its citizens are measured as accurately as possible on the scale of zero to one hundred in the belief, the identity, the social structure, the practice of innovation and project management as a culture in the society. By measurement, I mean to the percentage of people who adhere to this variable.

BELIEVE	is	Percentage of people who think their country can achieve greatness.
UNIFYING IDENTITY	is	Percentage of people that subscribe to a unifying identity or <u>accept</u> all partial identities as their own.
TRASH THE NEGATIVE SOCIAL STRUCTURES	is	Percentage of people who are aware of and are resisting all of the social structures such as Casts, Tribes, Race, and other divisive concepts and practices.
PRACTICE INNOVATION	is	Percentage of people aware of practice of innovation and use its techniques as a solid problem-solving approach to solve their personal, work, and social problems.
PRACTICE PM	is	Percentage of people who are aware of project management practice and practice it to varying degrees.
EVALUATE	is	The role of a person or a given entity to collect data, evaluate, and compile lessons.
REPEAT	is	Repeat to make sure that one person or country is progressing in all of the above.

STEP ONE

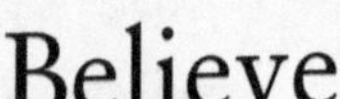

Believe

The believe rationale

This is as simple as the stereotype goes. You need to dream it, believe it, and then work hard to see it. The more nay-sayers we have, the less chance we will have people that work hard to make things happen.

BELIEVE THAT EVERYTHING IS POSSIBLE. I would define the "believe" factor as the number of the people in a given society or a larger gathering such as a country that answers the question, "do you answer the question that your country can achieve greatness, despite the status quo" with a YES. More specifically, they believe their country can produce results in defining a vision, setting up objectives, and working complex projects to achieve those objectives. The higher the percentage of the population, the faster the country can move forward.

STEP TWO

Unifying Identity

SEARCHING FOR A UNIFYING IDENTITY or Creating One. The lack of unifying identity is a DIRECT THREAT to partial identity and, by consequence, the country's existence as a whole. Having our own ethnic, regional, and neighborhood identity is important; however, we need to have a UNIFYING COUNTRY IDENTITY. If such an identity does not exist, we need to create one. We need to be aware that ignoring our own unifying identity is the most direct threat to our existence.

To start, the creation of a unifying identity starts with the members of the group being proud of what links the group together. I won't attempt to produce means that can diagnose or help in any way to lay the foundation for a unifying identity for any country, especially not Mauritania. This is due to my limited knowledge in social sciences, for one, and because it takes a considerable amount of time to model or method for this purpose for any social structure, let alone Mauritania. Nevertheless, since it seems that the pride which lay beneath every unifying identity is latent in a Story, I wanted to try to search for what is unique about one country, which I know best. Mauritania. This search hasn't taken a final form yet. But there is the foundation.

There are several ethnic groups in Mauritania, each with five casts or more. There are more than 500 tribes. The sum of these factors, however, makes my job a lot harder, I believe. As it turns out, I need to deal with more than several hundred groups with different interests. But let's not be discouraged and talk about the good things. Luckily, the majority of the tribes speak one language, and have only one religion. All the people practice Sunni Islam. Many think this is the identity of Mauritania. It is an important part of the identity of Mauritania, but it isn't enough. If it were, how come there is always tension? Tension between the tribes, the ethnic groups? We should not wait until a disaster happens, like it did in Rwanda, for the people to learn a lesson and for things to get better.

STEP THREE

Trashing the negative social structures

SOMETIMES I WISH I could tell my people, and I have done so on occasion, that the shoeless eight-year old's begging for change from across the window of your sometimes air-conditioned car is the possible 'criminal' who might hurt your grandson or your grandson's friend. If educated, the same eight-year-old could be the doctor who will cure your grandson of a killer disease.

I am not asking you to understand him and his generation of street beggars. I am not asking that you don't get annoyed with him and understand his needs. I am asking that you love the eight-year-old as you do, your son's friend. Avoiding eye contact out of guilt or shame you feel at that moment, feeling sorry for him that he is begging as a young, innocent child, or worse yet, crying while you disappear from his sight, will not do anything to change the social structure that "created" him in the first place.

That was a story of an encounter I had and wrote at the beginning of my drafting of this book. I was not sure where to place it. But as the book progressed, I knew there would be a place for this story in this section.

Any nation ought to be systematically aware of the social structures that improve or create injustice. The more people in the nation, country or tribe are aware of the dangers of negative or positive structures, the more likely it is for that nation to improve the positive ones and discard or change the negative. Some of the societal structures, be it tribal, caste, economic, racial, or otherwise historical, could be an important source of injustice. Injustice slows down progress. Injustice creeps into the foundation of the society and before we know it we will come to realize that the whole structure is under imminent threat of collapse. While governments around the world are hypnotized by and are proactive about GDP and APR known as growth domestic products and annual interest rates, they tend to be less so about injustice. I suggest the attention switches or become equal.

STEP FOUR

Practice Innovation!

It is simpler than you think!

WORRY NOT TOO MUCH ABOUT INNOVATION. Making innovation happen is simpler than you might think, and it is not always related to technology. Leaders and their governments often forget this fact. They, too, attempt to solve problems using the Books, and by books, I mean conventional methods. Put pressure on the ministers, spend money on national and international consulting, in the case of our country, copy, and paste. Copy and paste from the neighbors and when they want to show they have tried their best, from France. It never works.

It never works satisfactorily because it forgets to take into account what is unknown about the problem, the country, the neighbors, and for sure what is unknown by the experts in their problem savvy domain.

What do experts and consultants do when they are faced with what I'd like to call dark areas of knowledge? When there is no solution? They succumb to research. Research and research and development are slow to come up with a solution, and when it does, more often than not, it is expensive when its results are new. To put this into perspective and help make you believe that the practice of innovation is easy, let me outline the story of knowledge and ignorance and their relationship with awareness.

It has been said that in regards to knowledge and ignorance, there are things we know, and we think we know. Then there are things that we know, but we do not know that we know them (forgetfulness). And then lastly, there are things we do not know and are not aware that we do not know them. The worst is the last one: The things we do not know, and we are not aware of our ignorance of these things. Innovation is helpful in the last two. It is helpful to find solutions for the problems for which we have some or no knowledge, but we know that we have no way to find the knowledge to solve them. It is also useful we have total ignorance but we know we are not aware of that fact.

PRACTICING THE PROCESSES OF INNOVATION, such as idea generation methods and design thinking methods, are the shortcut to development and bypassing temporary ignorance being tackled by the research. I believe that countries should practice innovation while research and research and development do their job of lighting up the so-called dark areas of knowledge.

At the academic level, let us notice that there is a difference between creativity, invention, and innovation. One might invent a product or a service creatively, but only when they can do that continuously, are they called innovators.

I'd like to argue that only when innovation becomes a culture when society is more prone to risk-taking, is society likely to move forward. This culture needs to be taught at schools, community centers, colleges and universities, training centers, and be present in the media. It goes something like this:

1. Make sure the challenge or problem at hand hasn't been solved before and that there isn't an apparent solution in the books.
2. Specify the challenge with written words -- in the case of groups; it might be existent only in their collective consciousness.
3. Practice individual or group idea generation techniques to solve it.
4. If the sought after solution doesn't emerge, then revisit #1.
5. Apply the solution and learn from mistakes for the sake of improvement.

Mauritanians are known to innovate. How could it be possible to live in such harsh land isolated from the rest of the world for centuries and survive without innovation?

We innovated to build shelter, to eat, treat our sick, and to fight colonialism by inventing firearms from local materials only. Lest we believe, though, our innovation will not lead us with the necessary direction and speeds to move forward as a nation.

STEP FIVE

Practice Project Management

Spread the culture of standardized high-level steps of
Project Management according to Project Management
Institute.

THE MORE SPREAD OUT THE CULTURE OF PROJECT
MANAGEMENT, the less individual, group, and more
extensive government projects will fail. Innovation and
Project Management skills are integral to becoming the
new norm, lowering the computer divide challenge.

Now, notice that I used the abbreviations of PM and PMI.
I did so on purpose because let's try and avoid the common
misunderstanding of project management. Understanding
and practicing the basic principles of Project Management
Institute will make it possible to apply an algorithm that
has been studied time and again and design to minimize
risks, accomplish projects and programs on budget and on
time. Two well-known standards of project management

can be simplified to benefit the masses and be practiced at all levels. Project Management Body of Knowledge and Projects in Controlled Environments. The PMBOK of PMI and PRINCE 2. These two need to be **known** far and wide or shall I say we are popular as the social media platforms such as FB, Twitter, SnapChat, WhatsApp. MPI, PMP, PRINCE2.

PM Process of PMI

1	Project Initiation	What you need to do to start the project
2	Planning	List of activities, human, and material resources necessary to do the activities outlined in the time necessary to get the project done
3	Execution	Planned work is executed here
4	Monitoring	Monitoring
5	Closing	Closing and documenting lessons

STEP SIX & SEVEN

Evaluate & Repeat

COLLECTING DATA, EVALUATING RESULTS, and keeping things going with regards to the above six indicators is the government's job. However, any company or individual can do it. If governments and private sectors monitor economic indicators such as the market, why should they not monitor the belief indicator, the unifying indicators, social injustices, innovation, and project management indicators?

Epilogue

WITH MAURITANIA and other African nations being plugged in with the rest of the world to fiber optics cables, it has become more feasible for us to grow faster than ever before. Like it or not, know-how will be "downloaded" to Mauritania. The approach I presented in this book, an algorithm that can be used to develop countries, is prone to controversy. I know. It took me four years to finish the manuscript. One reason is procrastination, but one is my initial doubt in the method. In the end, though, I became convinced. You must have seen why in the book. Whether you agree with me fully or partially or not at all, I hope that the book will be a small contribution to the mess of ways and methods used to measure how well a country has moved forward.

About the author

Sidi holds a Ph.D. in mathematical and information science. His background (before the Ph.D.) is in computer science. Dr. Sidi graduated from Saitama University Japan in 2000 then worked at The Motorola Australian Research Center in Sydney. He taught and did some research in higher education in the US. He is the chairman of the US Mauritania Business Forum. He is now living in Mauritania, where he founded and managed a training and innovation institute (www.mifitt.net). He speaks several languages, including French, Arabic, English, and Japanese.

Sidi is interested in Mysticism, especially Sufism. He frequently reads the texts of Rumi & Ibn Arabi and biographies of other Sufi masters in the different Tariqas such as Naqshbendiya, Chadilillya, and Tijaniyya. Also, Dr. Sidi is passionate about helping poor African countries move ahead. This is the main reason he founded the institute and wrote this book.

About MiFiTT Institute

www.mifitt.net